S0-ASH-101

ADVERSITY

"When thou passest
through the waters, I will
be with thee; and through
the rivers, they shall not
overflow thee: when thou
walkest through the fire,
thou shalt not be burned;
neither shall the flame
kindle upon thee."

—Isaiah 43:2
The Holy Bible

"The Size Of Your Enemy Determines
The Size Of Your Reward."

—MIKE MURDOCK

- 1 -

2

ATTITUDE

"A merry heart doeth good like a medicine: but a broken spirit drieth the bones."

–Proverbs 17:22
The Holy Bible

"The Attitude Of The Servant Determines The Atmosphere Of The Palace."

-MIKE MURDOCK

3

CONTRACTS

"Can two walk together, except they be agreed?"

–Amos 3:3
The Holy Bible

"Those Unwilling To Discern Your Integrity Are Unqualified For Relationship."

-MIKE MURDOCK

4

CRISIS

"The Lord is my light and my salvation; whom shall I fear? the Lord is the strength of my life; of whom shall I be afraid?"

–Psalm 27:1
(See also Psalm 46:1-3)
The Holy Bible

"Crisis Always Occurs At The Curve Of Change."

-MIKE MURDOCK

5

DECISION-MAKING

"Trust in the Lord with all thine heart; and lean not unto thine own understanding. In all thy ways acknowledge Him, and He shall direct thy paths."

–Proverbs 3:5,6
The Holy Bible

"Those Without Your Goals May Never Understand Your Decisions."
-MIKE MURDOCK

DISCRETION

"A good man sheweth favour, and lendeth: he will guide his affairs with discretion."

–Psalm 112:5
The Holy Bible

"Never Discuss A Problem With Someone Incapable Of Solving It."
-MIKE MURDOCK

7

ECONOMY

"He shall not be afraid of evil tidings: his heart is fixed, trusting in the Lord."

–Psalm 112:7
The Holy Bible

"Every Step Towards Self-Sufficiency Is A Step Away From God."

-MIKE MURDOCK

8

FAMILY

"Thy wife shall be as a fruitful vine by the sides of thine house: thy children like olive plants round about thy table."

–Psalm 128:3
(See also Proverbs 18:22; 19:14; Ecclesiastes 9:9)

The Holy Bible

"The Proof Of Your Love Is The Passion To Pleasure."

-MIKE MURDOCK

9

FAVOR

"For Thou, Lord, wilt bless the righteous; with favour wilt Thou compass him as with a shield."

-Psalm 5:12
The Holy Bible

"One Day Of Favor Is Worth A Lifetime Of Labor."

-MIKE MURDOCK

10

FEAR OF GOD

"The fear of the Lord is the beginning of wisdom: a good understanding have all they that do His commandments: His praise endureth for ever."

–Psalm 111:10
(See also Proverbs 9:10)
The Holy Bible

"Your Respect Towards People Reveals Your Fear Of God."

-MIKE MURDOCK

11

GOAL-SETTING

" Write the vision, and make it plain upon tables, that he may run that readeth it. For the vision is yet for an appointed time, but at the end it shall speak, and not lie: though it tarry, wait for it; because it will surely come, it will not tarry."

–Habakkuk 2:2,3
The Holy Bible

"The Clearer Your Goal—The Greater Your Faith."

-MIKE MURDOCK

12

HOLY SPIRIT

"But ye shall receive power, after that the Holy Ghost is come upon you: and ye shall be witnesses unto Me both in Jerusalem, and in all Judaea, and in Samaria, and unto the uttermost part of the earth."

–Acts 1:8
The Holy Bible

"The Holy Spirit Is The Only Person Capable Of Being Contented With You."

-MIKE MURDOCK

13

LOSS

"And I will restore to you the years that the locust hath eaten, the cankerworm, and the caterpillar, and the palmerworm, my great army which I sent among you. And ye shall eat in plenty, and be satisfied, and praise the name of the Lord your God, that hath dealt wondrously with you: and My people shall never be ashamed."

-Joel 2:25,26

The Holy Bible

"The Quickest Cure For Ingratitude Is Loss."

-MIKE MURDOCK

14

MENTORSHIP

"The way of a fool is right in his own eyes: but he that hearkeneth unto counsel is wise."

–Proverbs 12:15
(See Proverbs 11:14; 24:6)
The Holy Bible

"There Are Two Ways To Get Wisdom—Mistakes And Mentors."
-MIKE MURDOCK

15

NEGOTIATION

"A soft answer turneth away wrath: but grievous words stir up anger."

–Proverbs 15:1
The Holy Bible

"Nothing Is Ever As It First Appears."
-MIKE MURDOCK

16

OBEDIENCE

"If ye be willing and obedient, ye shall eat the good of the land:"

–Isaiah 1:19
The Holy Bible

"The Instruction You Follow Determines The Future You Create."
-MIKE MURDOCK

17

OVERCOMING

"Wherefore take unto you the whole armour of God, that ye may be able to withstand in the evil day, and having done all, to stand."

–Ephesians 6:13
The Holy Bible

"What You Fail To Conquer Will Eventually Conquer You."

-MIKE MURDOCK

- 17 -

18

PRAYER

"Praying always with all prayer and supplication in the Spirit, and watching thereunto with all perseverance and supplication for all saints;"

–Ephesians 6:18
The Holy Bible

"The Proof Of Humility Is The Willingness To Reach."

-MIKE MURDOCK

- 18 -

19

PROBLEM-SOLVING

"Knowing that whatsoever good thing any man doeth, the same shall he receive of the Lord, whether he be bond or free."

–Ephesians 6:8
The Holy Bible

"The Problem You Solve Determines The Reward You Receive."

-MIKE MURDOCK

- 19 -

20

PROMOTION

"For promotion cometh neither from the east, nor from the west, nor from the south. But God is the judge: He putteth down one, and setteth up another."

–Psalm 75:6,7
(See also 1 Peter 5:6)
The Holy Bible

"You Can Only Be Promoted By The Person Whose Instruction You Follow."   -MIKE MURDOCK

- 20 -

21

PROSPERITY

"Let them shout for joy, and be glad, that favour My righteous cause: yea, let them say continually, Let the Lord be magnified, which hath pleasure in the prosperity of His servant."

–Psalm 35:27
(See also 3 John 2;
Deuteronomy 8:18)
The Holy Bible

"Prosperity Is Having Enough Of God's Provision To Complete His Instructions For Your Life."

-MIKE MURDOCK

- 21 -

22

PROTECTION

"There shall no evil befall thee, neither shall any plague come nigh thy dwelling. For He shall give His angels charge over thee, to keep thee in all thy ways."

–Psalm 91:10,11
The Holy Bible

"Your Willingness To Submit Authorizes God To Protect."

-MIKE MURDOCK

23

SELF-CONFIDENCE

"I can do all things through Christ which strengtheneth me."

–Philippians 4:13
The Holy Bible

"Your Similarity To Another Creates Your Comfort, Your Difference From Another Creates Your Confidence."

-MIKE MURDOCK

24

SOWING

"Give, and it shall be given unto you; good measure, pressed down, and shaken together, and running over, shall men give into your bosom. For with the same measure that ye mete withal it shall be measured to you again."

–Luke 6:38
The Holy Bible

"An Uncommon Seed Always Creates An Uncommon Harvest."

-MIKE MURDOCK

25

SUCCESS

"This book of the law shall not depart out of thy mouth; but thou shalt meditate therein day and night, that thou mayest observe to do according to all that is written therein: for then thou shalt make thy way prosperous, and then thou shalt have good success."

–Joshua 1:8
The Holy Bible

"Your Success Depends On The Problems You Are Willing To Solve For Others."

-MIKE MURDOCK

26

TIME-MANAGEMENT

"To every thing there is a season, and a time to every purpose under the heaven:"

—Ecclesiastes 3:1
(See also Ecclesiastes 3:2-8)
The Holy Bible

"Joy Is The Reward For Discerning The Divine Product Of The Immediate Moment."

-MIKE MURDOCK

- 26 -

27

TITHING

"Bring ye all the tithes into the storehouse, that there may be meat in Mine house, and prove Me now herewith, saith the Lord of hosts, if I will not open you the windows of heaven, and pour you out a blessing, that there shall not be room enough to receive it. And I will rebuke the devourer for your sakes, and he shall not destroy the fruits of your ground; neither shall your vine cast her fruit before the time in the field, saith the Lord of hosts."

–Malachi 3:10,11

The Holy Bible

"Tithing Is Returning To God That Which Does Not Belong To You."

-MIKE MURDOCK

28

WISDOM

"Wisdom is the principal thing; therefore get wisdom: and with all thy getting get understanding."
–Proverbs 4:7
The Holy Bible

"Wisdom Is The Scriptural Solution To Your Most Immediate Problem." -MIKE MURDOCK

29

WORD OF GOD

"Thou through Thy commandments hast made me wiser than mine enemies: for they are ever with me."
–Psalm 119:98
The Holy Bible

"The Power Of God In Your Life Is Never Proportionate To Your Need Of Him But Proportionate To Your Knowledge Of Him."
-MIKE MURDOCK

30

WORDS

"Pleasant words are as an honeycomb, sweet to the soul, and health to the bones."

–Proverbs 16:24
The Holy Bible

"What You Say Determines What Others Feel."

-MIKE MURDOCK

- 29 -

31

WORK

"Every man also to whom God hath given riches and wealth, and hath given him power to eat thereof, and to take his portion, and to rejoice in his labour; this is the gift of God."

–Ecclesiastes 5:19
The Holy Bible

"What You Love Most Is A Clue To The Gifts You Contain."

-MIKE MURDOCK

DECISION

Will You Accept Jesus As Your Personal Savior Today?

The Bible says, "That if thou shalt confess with thy mouth the Lord Jesus, and shalt believe in thine heart that God hath raised Him from the dead, thou shalt be saved" (Romans 10:9).

Pray this prayer from your heart today! *"Dear Jesus, I believe that You died for me and rose again on the third day. I confess I am a sinner...I need Your love and forgiveness...Come into my heart. Forgive my sins. I receive Your eternal life. Confirm Your love by giving me peace, joy and supernatural love for others. Amen."*

☐ Yes, Mike! I made a decision to accept Christ as my personal Savior today. Please send me my free gift of your book *"31 Keys to a New Beginning"* to help me with my new life in Christ. *(B-48)*

NAME _____

ADDRESS _____

CITY _____ STATE _____ ZIP _____

PHONE ( ) _____ EMAIL _____

Mail To: **The Wisdom Center** *(B-141)*
P.O. Box 99 · Denton, TX 76202
1-888-WISDOM-1 (1-888-947-3661)
Website: www.thewisdomcenter.tv

Unless otherwise indicated, all Scripture quotations are taken from the King James Version of the Bible.
31 Scriptures Every Businessman Should Memorize · ISBN 1-56394-266-6/B-141
Copyright © 2003 by **MIKE MURDOCK**
All publishing rights belong exclusively to Wisdom International
Published by The Wisdom Center · P.O. Box 99 · Denton, Texas 76202
1-888-WISDOM-1 (1-888-947-3661) · **Website: www.thewisdomcenter.tv**
Printed in the United States of America. All rights reserved under International Copyright Law. Contents and/or cover may not be reproduced in whole or in part in any form without the expressed written consent of the publisher. 1103◊100k